Some materials look the same.
Which bottle is made from glass?

Can you think of some more things made of plastic?
Can you think of some more things made of glass?

We can group materials by their **properties**.

Which material can you see through?

plastic

glass

Materials

Some of these things are made from metal.

Some of these things are made from wood.

How many different groups of materials can you see?

Lots of bark chippings have been put around this playground.

6

What is wrong with these things?

How many different materials can you see in this bathroom?

 **Why have these materials been used in a bathroom?**

Changing materials can make them useful.

1

2

3

spinning

4

Look at these pictures.
What happens to the sheep's
wool to make knitting wool?

Bark chippings stop weeds growing around plants.

Can you think of more materials that can be used in different ways?

The knitting wool can be made into a jumper.

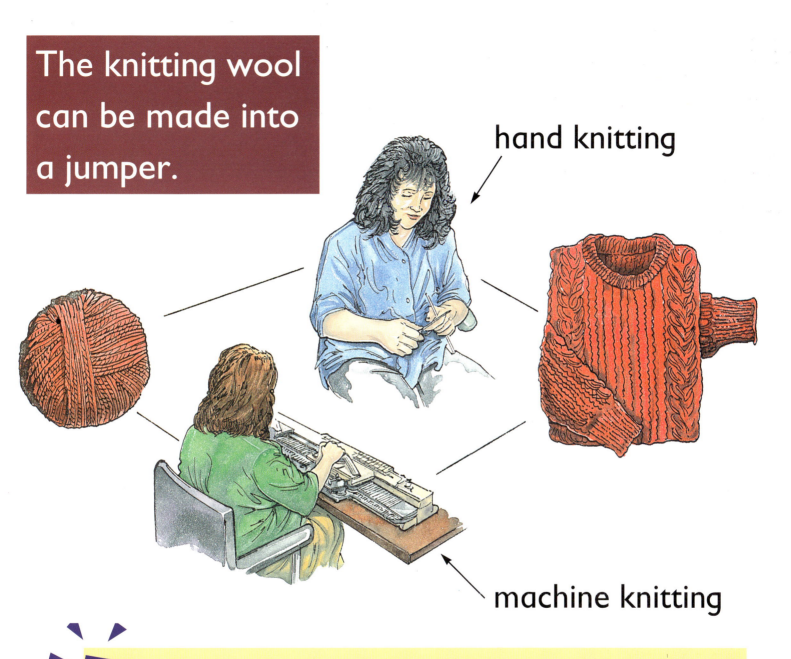

hand knitting

machine knitting

Can you think of some more ways to change materials?

Help Jack to find materials for:

1 Changing the colour of a door

2 Making a bird table

3 Mending a broken window

4 Decorating a bedroom

5 Making a garden fence.